DATE DUE

	FEB 1 4 2011		

DEMCO 38-296

DRUGS AND YOUR FRIENDS

Friends must make choices about following the examples of their peers.

THE DRUG ABUSE PREVENTION LIBRARY

DRUGS AND YOUR FRIENDS

Sue Hurwitz and Nancy Shniderman

THE ROSEN PUBLISHING GROUP, INC.
NEW YORK

To Gene
S.H.
To Jeff
N.S.
And a special thank you to:
James J. Khalili, Ph.D.
Psychological Development Services Olathe, Kansas,
and
The Kansas Department of Social and Rehabilitation Services:
Alcohol and Drug Abuse Services
Topeka, Kansas

The people pictured in this book are only models; they, in no way, practice or endorse the activities illustrated. Captions serve only to explain the subjects of photographs and do not in any way imply a connection between the real-life models and the staged situations shown.

Published in 1992, 1993 by The Rosen Publishing Group, Inc.
29 East 21st Street, New York, NY 10010

Revised Edition 1993

Copyright © 1992, 1993 by The Rosen Publishing Group, Inc.

Printed in Canada

Library of Congress Cataloging-in-Publication Data

Hurwitz, Sue
    Drugs and your friends/by Sue Hurwitz and Nancy
    Shniderman.
    (The Drug Abuse Prevention Library)
    Includes bibliographical references and index.
    Summary: Discusses peer pressure and drug use and the
    importance of making the right choice.
        ISBN 0-8239-1657-X
        1. Teenagers—United States—Drug use—Juvenile lit-
    erature.2. Teenagers—United States—Alcohol use—
    Juvenile literature. 3. Children—United States—Drug
    use, Juvenile literature. 4. Children—United States—
    Alcohol use—Juvenile literature.
    [1. Drug use. 2. Substance abuse.]
    I. Shniderman, Nancy, 1956-. II. Title III. Series
    HV5824. Y68H87   1991
    362.29'083—dc20
                        90-913
                        CIP
                        AC

Contents

Introduction

You have to make many choices in life. Some are more difficult than others. Some are better than others. Choosing to stay home on Saturday night to study for an exam on Monday is tough, but a good choice. Choosing to hang out in a parking lot, drinking beer with your friends on Friday night after the football game is not a good choice. Drinking alcohol is illegal for anyone under the age of 21. It is harmful to your body, and it often results in dangerous, if not fatal, behavior.

Going to a party can be a great choice, especially if the guy or girl you've been dying to meet all year is there. Smoking cigarettes or pot at that party is not a good choice. Tobacco and marijuana are both addictive. They both can cause cancer. Neither of them is good for your body or your mind.

Today you face more choices than ever. Ask your parents. They'll tell you they never had to make the kinds of choices about using drugs that you have to make.

Cocaine, crack, heroin, marijuana, tobacco, and alcohol are all drugs. Today they are very common among teenagers. Maybe even among your friends. It is likely that you will have to decide whether or not to try any of the drugs mentioned above, or even some that aren't mentioned. You may already have had to decide.

Like any choice, deciding whether or not to use drugs must be based on good information. That is what this book is all about: good information. Sometimes you don't have time to get that information. Sometimes you are pressured by your friends to decide. This book looks at how your friends can help you make good or bad choices. It discusses how you can say no to friends who try to control you.

You have to make your own choices if you want to control your own life. That is your *right*. This book will give you good information about drugs and your friends. It will help you make good choices.

But the decisions are up to you. And what happens because of your decisions is also up to you.

Liquor is legal for adults and easy to get—but is an illegal drug for teenagers.

CHAPTER 1

Drugs—What They Are and What They Do

You see drugs used on TV shows and in movies. You see ads for alcohol or tobacco in magazines and newspapers. You may see people smoke, drink, or use drugs. You may see someone sell drugs. You may know someone who does it.

Using alcohol, tobacco, and drugs looks like fun. It looks grown-up. It looks like something to do. You may be curious.

But do you really know about drugs and what they do? Will someone who sells drugs or alcohol or tobacco really tell you that they are harmful?

A drug is a chemical that causes changes in the way you feel and think and behave. Some drugs are healthful. Those

10 | drugs are called medicines. It is not against the law to buy them or to use them. It is also not illegal for pharmacists to sell them.

This chapter is about some drugs that are harmful and illegal. It also describes some drugs that are not illegal but are harmful.

Alcohol

Alcohol is the number one drug problem for young people in America today. In 1985, about 4.5 million young people between the ages of 14 and 17 were involved in alcohol-related problems. Many were arrested. Many were involved in accidents including drowning and fires.

Alcohol kills about 98,000 people each year. More than half of them die in auto accidents.

Alcohol is easy to get. Alcohol is not illegal to buy or to use for people over a certain age. But alcohol is *always* harmful. The younger you are, the more harmful it is to drink.

About 10 million people in the United States depend on alcohol. These people are called *alcoholics*. They find it hard or impossible to do without alcohol. They are *hooked*. Alcohol can easily become habit-forming. Some teenagers become alcoholics less than six months after taking their first drink.

Alcohol is a chemical formed by fermenting the sugar in grains or fruits. The kind of alcohol found in beer and wine is called ethyl alcohol. Ethyl alcohol is also found in hard liquors such as whiskey, gin, vodka, and brandy.

Alcohol is a mind-changing drug just like cocaine or crack. It takes only about fifteen minutes for alcohol to travel through your bloodstream to your brain. Alcohol depresses or slows down your *central nervous system.* The central nervous system controls the way you stand, walk, and speak. Alcohol also slows down muscle movement.

At first a drinker may feel relaxed. A drinker may get a feeling of pleasure called a "high." But then the drinker begins to lose self-control. He or she may not think clearly enough to make good choices. He or she may take unnecessary risks or say or do things he or she is sorry for later. The drinker may talk loudly and become abusive. The drinker may become clumsy.

Long-term drinking can damage your brain. It can also damage your liver,

12 | kidneys, heart, and stomach. Alcohol can cause skin problems and diarrhea.

But you don't need to be an alcoholic to have serious problems from drinking. Even one drink can give you a pounding headache, or *hangover.* One drink can make you vomit—or wish you could! One drink can cause you to fall and hurt yourself. One drink can make you reckless and get you into trouble with others or the law. Even one drink can cause you to have an auto accident and maybe kill yourself or others.

Even one drink is too many.

Even one drink is illegal.

Tobacco

About one million teenagers and children in the United States start smoking every year. Every state has laws saying a person must be over a certain age to buy and to use cigarettes. Almost everyone knows that tobacco and tobacco smoke are harmful to your health.

But many people still make poor choices. Many people still smoke cigarettes, cigars, or pipes. Some teenagers also use *snuff* in their nose or chew tobacco even though tobacco is harmful and illegal.

A teenager who starts smoking cigarettes is making a very poor choice.

14   Nicotine is a colorless, oily chemical in tobacco. Nicotine is habit-forming and makes it hard to stop smoking once you start. Smokers quickly become used to having nicotine in their body and they crave it. Nicotine is a poison that is used as a weed killer. Large doses of nicotine can kill you.

Nicotine travels from your lungs into your bloodstream in seconds. It speeds up your heart and nervous system. Nicotine also slows down the amount of blood that reaches your heart. And that is harmful.

Smokers say that smoking helps them relax. But they also complain of sore throats, coughing, shortness of breath, and dulled sense of taste.

Carbon monoxide is a gas in the fumes that come out of a car's exhaust pipe. Carbon monoxide is also in cigarette smoke. It is dangerous to the smoker. It is also dangerous to nonsmokers who are near someone smoking.

Tar is a cancer-causing chemical in tobacco. Tar is the brownish, sticky stuff that smokers get on their fingers and ashtrays. Tar is made of several hundred different chemicals. It can damage a smoker's lungs when it is inhaled with cigarette smoke.

Smoking cigarettes greatly increases the 15
risk of many kinds of cancer. Lung cancer
is ten times more frequent in smokers
than in nonsmokers. But a year after a
smoker stops smoking, the risk of lung
cancer is greatly reduced.

Smoking tobacco also increases the risk
of cancer of the mouth, throat, voice box,
and esophagus (the tube from your mouth
to your stomach). Both bladder and kid-
ney cancer are related to tobacco smoking.

Smoking in America dates back to before Christopher Columbus arrived here in
1492. American natives showed Columbus
how to roll tobacco leaves and smoke
them. Columbus took the habit back to
Europe.

In those days, people didn't know how
harmful it was to smoke. But now we do.
Now nonsmokers don't want to breathe
the carbon monoxide from smokers' cigarettes. More and more public places limit
where smokers may smoke. Warnings are
printed on the packages of cigarettes. It is
no longer "cool" to smoke. Smokers are
less and less welcome.

Today everyone knows that cigarette
smoke is dangerous. Many places will not
hire people who smoke, or will allow them
to smoke only in certain areas. A smoker

16 is becoming more and more limited in his or her choices.

The best choice a smoker can make is to stop smoking!

Marijuana

Marijuana is also called "grass" or "pot." Marijuana is made from a plant called *Cannabis sativa.* It contains more than 400 chemicals. THC, tetrahydrocannabinol, is the main chemical in marijuana. The more THC in a cigarette or *joint,* the greater the high. There is more THC in today's marijuana than in past years. So there is greater harm in smoking it either in a cigarette or a pipe.

At first a smoker may feel relaxed and silly. But after a while the user becomes sleepy.

Marijuana increases your pulse rate and makes your eyes bloodshot. Your mouth becomes dry. Marijuana affects your brain, making it hard to concentrate. Marijuana also affects your sense of timing and muscle movement, making it dangerous to drive after smoking.

Some users have panic attacks and fear "losing control." Long-term use of marijuana also makes a user lose interest in

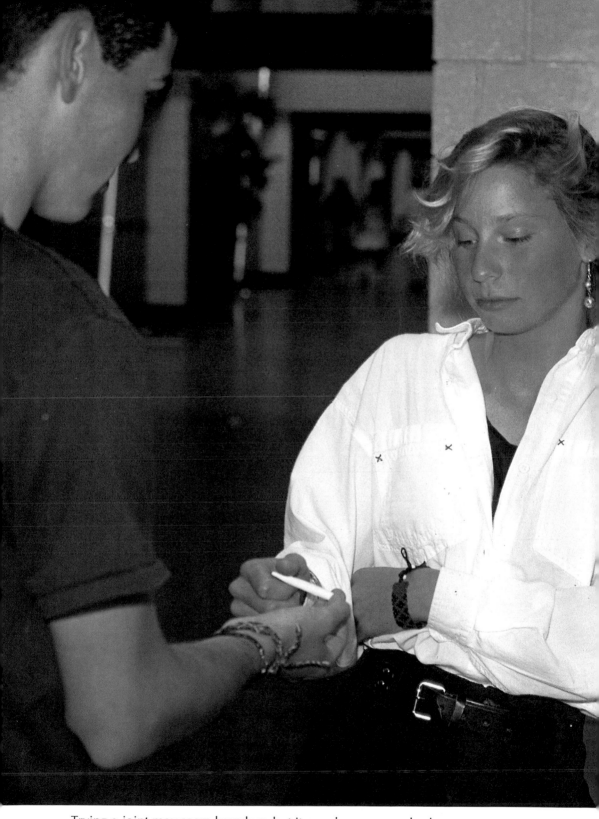

Trying a joint may seem harmless, but it can damage your body and your mind.

18 life. That leads to learning problems at school and makes it hard to keep a job.

Marijuana smoke contains even more cancer-causing chemicals than tobacco smoke and is dangerous to a smoker's lungs. And smoking tobacco and marijuana together is even more harmful.

Marijuana is stored in the fatty parts of body cells. Since one third of your brain has these fatty cells, it takes a long time for marijuana to leave the body. The chemicals from a single joint can take a month to leave a smoker's body even though the smoker felt the high for only a few hours.

Drug abuse often starts with alcohol, tobacco, or marijuana use. These three drugs are called "gateway" drugs because they often lead to use of other drugs. When young people use these drugs to avoid facing the problems of growing up they are more likely to try other drugs too.

Cocaine and Crack

Cocaine is a drug made from leaves of the coca plant, which grows in South America. Cocaine is usually made into a fine white crystal-like powder. When the powder is

You can say "no" to friends who offer you crack or other drugs.

Drug-addicted teens may steal from friends to buy their next fix.

sniffed or *snorted* into the nose it is absorbed into the user's blood Cocaine can also be injected, or shot into a user's vein.

Crack is a form of cocaine that is made into large white crystals. Crack is smoked, or *freebased*. When crack is absorbed into a user's lungs, the effects are usually felt within a few seconds.

The crack high is more powerful than the cocaine high. The crack high lasts five or ten minutes. It is followed by a powerful *crash*, or withdrawal symptoms. This leaves the user tired, depressed, and irritable. That is what makes crack so habit-forming. The user wants more crack right away to avoid these bad feelings.

Users become dependent on crack from the first time or two they use it. After trying crack only once, a person may be hooked.

Cocaine and crack affect the body in the same way, but the effects of crack are faster. The user's heartbeat speeds up greatly. Blood vessels tighten, and that raises the user's blood pressure. Pupils of the eyes dilate. Less oxygen reaches the brain. This can result in mental problems and in stroke. Cocaine users also run the risk of having fluids settle in their lungs.

An evening of drinking, doing drugs, and driving can lead to a terrible injury or even death.

24 If the cocaine, or "coke," is snorted, the chemical damages the lining of the user's nose.

Cocaine is also harmful to the reproductive systems of men and women. During pregnancy cocaine use can cut off oxygen to the unborn child. The child may be born addicted to cocaine and die.

We all have heard of famous people who died from using cocaine and crack. These deaths are not usually from an overdose but because coke and crack are absorbed so quickly by the body. The increased heartbeat causes a heart attack.

No one can tell how his or her body may react to a drug. Some people may get by for a long time without a bad reaction. But some people die from trying crack only once.

Heroin

Heroin is a drug made from opium, which comes from a poppy plant grown in the warm climates of Asia. Heroin is made into a white powder that may be inhaled or injected.

When heroin is injected into a vein, the user risks damaged veins and sores and needle marks on his or her arms. If a user shares a needle or uses a dirty needle there is the added risk of infection or catching *AIDS*.

Heroin gives the user a powerful high followed by a feeling of relaxation. But it soon takes more and more of the drug to reach the high. The heroin is taken not for the pleasure of the high but to avoid the bad feelings of the crash.

Someone using heroin has a slower heart rate and shallow breathing. A user may become restless, drowsy, or feel like vomiting. During the crash the user may have painful cramps, diarrhea, chills, or sweating for a week or more.

The effects of heroin last three to six hours. During this time the user keeps wanting more and more heroin. There is a big danger of overdosing during this period.

Is using drugs really worth the risk?

Do you really think a mature person would harm his or her body and mind that way?

That is something you need to think about when you make your choice about drugs.

That is something you need to remember when your friends try to make your drug choices for you.

A drinking habit can lead to a lonely life as the addict loses friends and relationships.

CHAPTER 2

Friends and Peer Pressure

James's Friends Use Alcohol

"So, James, it's about time you showed up at one of my parties." Scott smiled and put his arm around James, pulling him into the living room.

"Yeah, I know." James knew about Scott's parties. Scott had been his best friend in elementary school. Once they got older, Scott made other friends. James had heard that Scott's new friends drank a lot. It wasn't James's scene, but he decided to see what Scott was up to.

Scott's parents were divorced. He lived with his father, but his dad was often away on business trips. It was the perfect place for a party. Scott became one of the most popular kids in school. He and James were still friends, but not very close. James missed the friendship they'd had.

28

"Here, have a beer." Scott shoved his can into James's hand and went to the kitchen to grab another beer for himself. James was caught off guard. "Hey, man, I don't drink. I don't want this."

He looked around the living room to see who was there. He saw Scott's friends Pete and Greg in the corner talking to two girls. They were all drunk. The girls were laughing at a story Pete was telling. One of them laughed so hard she lost her balance. She fell against Greg, who tried to catch her. He missed, and they both fell.

James spotted a girl he didn't know. She was flipping through a magazine she'd found somewhere and drinking a soda. She looked bored. James started toward her, but was cut off by Greg stumbling for the bathroom. Greg didn't make it. He threw up just outside the bathroom door. James made a face and kept walking.

"Hi, there. Where'd you get the soda?" he asked.

"There's some hiding in the kitchen, but you have to look really hard." Katie looked up and smiled. She had noticed James in school and thought he was good-looking. But when she saw the beer in his hand, she'd written him off as another jerk. Now she was pleasantly surprised.

Peers can pressure you to do drugs or drink—but a good friend can give advice and comfort you when you're feeling down.

30

"I think I'll go trade this in." James set the beer down on a table.

"I'll help you find the soda. By the way, I'm Katie." James introduced himself, and helped Katie up. They went into the crowded kitchen. Katie squeezed between two people in a chugging contest and grabbed two sodas.

"I hate to drink," James said. "I don't like to lose control of myself."

"Yeah, beer has a way of messing up your mind," Katie agreed.

Just then Scott staggered in. "James, where's your beer? Isn't that what you came for?" Scott's words were slurred.

"No way, man. I came to see you and hang out with friends. I don't drink. This is fine with me," James held up his soda.

"Come on. Spice up your life a little." Scott grabbed an open bottle of rum from the counter and tried to pour some into James's soda. James set the can down. "Scott, I don't want to drink. I can't spare the brain cells. Come on, Katie. Let's go," he said.

"All right," Katie agreed. "I've had enough of this scene."

On their way out, James turned back to Scott and said, "Call me when you get tired of this."

Scott just waved his hand in disgust.

James walked Katie home. She told him a little about herself.

"I used to drink all the time. My mother's an alcoholic, too. I guess I take after her. I've stopped drinking, though, and go to Alateen now. I'm trying to persuade Mom to go to AA, you know, Alcoholics Anonymous."

"I don't know if Scott is an alcoholic, but maybe I should let him know about Alateen," said James.

"Scott's been throwing these parties for a while. I used to go to all of them. Now I only go once in a while. It's hard to be around them when they drink, but they're my friends so I hang out. I just stick to soda, though."

"Well, I'd consider us friends now. We could hang out," James said.

"I'm really glad I met you. It's nice to know that not everybody wants to get wasted." Katie stopped and smiled at James. "Thanks for walking me home. Maybe we could study together tomorrow or something?"

"That would be great. Let's meet at the library around four o'clock."

"I'll see you tomorrow, then. G'night." Katie turned and went into the house.

Cigarettes can be so habit-forming that addicts may have to sneak a smoke between other activities.

James made several good choices to avoid letting his peers involve him with alcohol. He said no to the first drink. He got himself a nonalcoholic drink. He and Katie discussed the effects of alcohol.

James tried two methods of avoiding peer pressure when Scott tried to spike his soda. First, he put down the soda. Second, he joked off the pressure.

Finally, James hoped to use positive peer pressure on Scott. Since Pete and Greg made bad choices for him, maybe he would let James make a good choice with the help of AA or Alateen.

Darcy's Friends Use Tobacco and Marijuana

When Rose called Darcy and asked her to go to Megan's slumber party, Darcy said "No."

"It will be fun, Darcy," Rose coaxed. Don't you want to see all our friends?" "I've been to Megan's parties before," Darcy said. "Kathy and Charla will probably chain-smoke all night!"

Darcy swallowed the lump in her throat as she suddenly remembered her grandmother. Grams was a heavy smoker and lived the last ten years of her life battling

34 | emphysema. Darcy remembered how Grams' lips turned blue from lack of oxygen. She remembered how Grams struggled for every breath. Darcy also remembered how Grams finally was dependent on an oxygen machine just to live a few years longer.

Darcy was not going to let that happen to her!

Grams' doctor had told her that addiction to nicotine was harder to beat than addiction to most other drugs. The doctor was right. Grams tried many, many times to stop smoking. But she couldn't stop even though her life depended on it.

"I know you don't approve of smoking," Rose said. "But just because other people smoke doesn't mean we have to."

"I don't even want to be around it. It smells disgusting, and secondhand smoke is just as bad for you as smoking the cigarette yourself. I just can't stand to think that I might end up like Grams," Darcy added.

Rose sighed. "Oh, Darcy, be a sport. You and Megan are the only ones who are old enough to drive. Why don't you take me over to Megan's and see how things are going? If Charla and Kathy smoke as much as last time, you can leave. I'll call

Trying to kick a smoking habit is hard, but it's one of the best choices you can make.

36 my parents in the morning to come after me."

"Okay. But don't try to pressure me into staying if I decide not to, Rose. You know I make my own decisions."

"Agreed!"

Darcy and Rose were the first to arrive at Megan's house. They listened to music in Megan's room while they waited for Kathy and Charla. They talked about what they had been doing since school ended the month before.

Darcy was having a great time. She hoped Carla and Kathy had stopped smoking so much. She didn't want them to ruin the evening.

Darcy's hopes soon fell.

When Charla and Kathy strolled in, Charla was puffing on a cigarette. They sat down on the floor, and Kathy opened her purse. "We're really going to have a party tonight!" Kathy boasted. "I took some of my sister's pot!"

"I haven't had a joint in nearly a month!" Charla exclaimed. She blew three smoke rings into the air, then crushed out her cigarette. "I can't wait to get high!"

"I thought we were going to play cards or something," Rose reminded her friends.

"Are you two just going to sit around and smoke all night again?"

"Don't be a nag, Rose," Kathy complained with a sigh. "Grow up! Try this weed and relax a little." Kathy lit the marijuana and inhaled deeply. She closed her eyes and leaned back against the side of Megan's bed, handing the reefer to Rose.

"I'm not in the mood." Rose made an excuse and didn't reach for the marijuana cigarette.

But Megan did. She inhaled slightly, then began coughing. She immediately handed the grass to Charla.

Darcy was uncomfortable. She had planned to leave if her friends started using tobacco. Now that they were experimenting with marijuana, she was definitely leaving.

"I'm going," Darcy told Rose. "Do you want to come along and we'll stop for pizza?"

"You don't know what you're missing!" Kathy said as Darcy took the car keys from her purse.

"Oh, but I do!" Darcy responded. "I'm missing several kinds of cancer, heart disease, and emphysema!" Darcy turned to Rose. "What did you decide, Rose?"

38

"Pizza sounds good," Charla interrupted before Rose could reply. "Why don't we all go for pizza?"

"I'm sorry you don't want to stay, Darcy," Megan said sincerely. "But I understand. Maybe some other time?"

"Yeah," Darcy promised.

"Me, too," Rose echoed. "Maybe another time."

"Pizza does sound good," Megan decided. "Since you aren't coming back here, I'll drive and we'll meet you there."

"No, Megan. It's dangerous to drive after you've smoked pot. Your reactions are slower than normal. You could get into an accident. Why don't you ride with us? I'll take you back afterwards. You guys won't be normal for another twelve hours."

"Thanks, Darcy. We'd love to!" Kathy chimed in. "Let's go before Megan's parents find out that we've been smoking pot!"

"Yeah, let's!" Charla agreed between giggles.

"I don't know why I let Kathy tempt me into trying marijuana," Megan admitted later as they ate. "I know there are more cancer-causing chemicals in one joint than in a whole pack of cigarettes. I guess I was just curious."

Even if friends want you to drink, it's still your decision.

40   "You know, you really shouldn't mix drugs," Rose told Charla. "Tobacco and marijuana are both drugs. Mixing can be dangerous. Sometimes even deadly."

Charla didn't answer Rose. The marijuana high had worn off, but she couldn't concentrate on what Rose was saying.

"I'm going to try to cut down on smoking," Megan blurted out. "My cousin Gwen took a no-smoking class given at one of the hospitals. She stopped smoking in six weeks. I'll have a serious talk with Gwen and find out what else helped her quit."

"That sounds like a good choice," Darcy told Megan. "You might also check out no-smoking videos from the library."

Megan sighed. "Thanks for suggesting the pizza and getting us out of the house, Darcy. When you drop us at home, I'll insist that Kathy doesn't take any more marijuana out of her purse."

Later, as Darcy drove her friends back to Megan's house, she thought about the evening. The marijuana had made Kathy paranoid—she was afraid her sister would miss the joints or that Megan's parents would discover her drug use. Charla became silly and couldn't stop giggling. Megan felt guilty and probably would not experiment with drugs again. Rose felt relieved to get away from the peer pressure to use pot.

How did she feel? Darcy was sorry she had wasted the evening. She should have gone to a movie with Rose as they usually did on a Saturday night.

Darcy had a strong reason to avoid using tobacco. She had watched her grandmother die a slow death. She had vowed not to abuse her mind or body with drugs or tobacco. Because Darcy knew what was best for her, she wasn't influenced by her peers.

Darcy set limits before going to the party. She told Rose that she would leave if their friends used tobacco. When the situation occurred, Darcy knew exactly what to do. She didn't even need to think about making a choice.

Rose, Darcy's best friend, was also drug-free. But Rose was anxious to appear grown-up since she was one of the younger members of the group. Rose wasn't as assertive as Darcy when it came to resisting peer pressure. But she was learning.

Darcy suggested a different activity—to go for pizza—to help Rose get away from

Drug and alcohol abuse can make you violently ill.

peer pressure. Darcy showed Kathy that she knew the effects of smoking both tobacco and marijuana. Darcy made it clear that she chose not to use them.

When Darcy saw that Megan planned to drive, she offered to take everyone else along to keep Megan from driving after using drugs.

Finally, Darcy encouraged Megan to get advice from someone who had kicked the tobacco habit. She remembered that nicotine was so addictive that her grandmother never could stop smoking.

But Darcy hoped that Megan would!

Brad's Friends Use Cocaine and Crack

Brad's vision was still blurred. His muscles still twitched. He was so jittery that he could barely stay on the chair in the counselor's office. He felt like running out of the school. But that would only get him in deeper trouble.

"You know schools don't need search warrants to search students' lockers," Mr. Johnson explained.

Brad finally focused his attention on the counselor. He and Tony had just snorted all the cocaine they had bought earlier from a guy behind the school. He

44 wasn't worried that anything would be found in his locker.

"I know," Brad answered as he stared across the desk at Mr. Johnson.

"Are you aware that the federal Anti-Drug Abuse Act of 1986 made punishments for possessing or selling drugs much tougher?"

"Yes."

"Pushers and users aren't getting off with suspended sentences anymore. In the next few years punishments for offenders will get even tougher."

Brad didn't answer. He felt like puking. His coke was wearing off and he wondered if he would die. He almost wished he would. The crashes were so painful that he felt miserable just knowing what was ahead for him.

At least he hadn't smoked crack as Tony and his friends had wanted him to the night before. He had watched Tony's crack crash and it was unbearable!

"Urinalysis, the testing of urine to see if a person has used drugs, is a growing practice," Mr. Johnson continued. "Urinalysis is used not only by law enforcement officers but also by employers, schools, and colleges now."

"Umm." Brad knew about urinalysis.
There was no way to beat it. If you used
drugs and were tested, the book was
thrown at you. Everyone had heard about
athletes who lost jobs, titles, and medals
because they tested positive to a urinalysis.

"If drugs are found in your locker, you'll
be suspended from school." Mr. Johnson
cleared his throat. "A suspension from
high school for drug use could limit your
opportunities later for college or a job."

Brad didn't care. Tony had suffered a
bad reaction to the coke. After Brad had
gone to the office for help, Tony was taken
to the hospital. Unconscious. Maybe
dead. What did it matter if he was thrown
out of school? He couldn't say he deserved
better.

Mr. Johnson answered the buzz from
his intercom. Nothing illegal had been
found in Brad's locker. He was free to go.

But how free was Brad? Would his
close call with the law make him stop
using drugs? Would he remain a slave to
coke?

"Come in and see me if you ever feel
like talking," Mr. Johnson told Brad.
"Talking to someone about your problems
usually helps."

46

Brad sighed. "I'd like that, Mr. Johnson. I'll come in tomorrow. Right now I'm going to the hospital to see Tony."

The United States has the highest rate of teenage drug use in the industrialized world. Brad and Tony were part of that number.

When Tony was pressured to smoke crack the night before, Brad knew he was getting dragged deeper and deeper into a life-style that he didn't want. He claimed that his parents expected him home immediately. Then he left.

But Brad was wondering how to break the drug cycle. Now Mr. Johnson had given him an option.

Brad was ready to get help by talking to Mr. Johnson. He realized that drugs would ruin his future if he didn't stop now. He only hoped that Tony would be able to join him the next day.

Lee's Friends Use Heroin

Lee came from a good family. She didn't worry about money or clothes. She always had enough. But she didn't have any friends—either male or female. She didn't feel like she belonged at school. She was sad and lonely.

Making friends who are drug-free will help you stay that way too.

48 Paula, a girl in Lee's history class, asked if Lee wanted to go to a party with her cousin, Dale.

Lee was thrilled and agreed.

When Dale came to pick Lee up for the party, she noticed that he was very thin and coughed a lot. But he was friendly, and Lee enjoyed the attention.

At the party, Lee saw many people lying around looking sleepy. She was disappointed that the party wasn't more lively with people dancing and talking.

Soon, Dale asked Lee if she used heroin.

"Aren't you worried about AIDS?" Lee asked.

"I'm not stupid enough to *mainline*. I don't shoot up my veins," Dale boasted. "I roll junk inside a cigarette and smoke it!"

Dale "fixed" a cigarette with heroin and took a drag off it. Then he handed it to Lee. "Take a puff, Lee, " Dale coaxed. "It's fantastic!"

Lee was eager to be accepted into the group. She didn't think much about what might happen if she became dependent on heroin. So Lee began using heroin to please Dale. But she didn't find heroin fantastic at all.

Before long Lee was addicted to heroin. She was doing things she had never thought she'd do. She was lying to her parents. She was cutting classes to see Dale and get more heroin. The heroin left her too sleepy to do her homework. She often slept in class, too. Her grades dropped, and she was barely passing her classes.

When Lee was awake, she spent most of her time looking for more heroin. She began selling her clothes and jewelry to get money to help Dale buy junk, or smack.

Finally Lee's parents realized something was wrong. They insisted that Lee stop seeing Dale and her new friends. They also demanded that she get treatment for her addiction.

Lee knew she faced some difficult choices. She could fight her parents' advice and continue to see Dale and to use heroin. After all, she was almost fifteen. She didn't have to do everything her parents wanted her to do!

But she was even more unhappy now than she had been before she met Dale. Using heroin didn't solve Lee's low self-image problem. Heroin only added more

50 | problems to her life. It made her feel worthless.

Lee realized that she had not thought about what might happen when she began using heroin. Now she knew that saying "Yes" to heroin was a bad choice. Lee knew she needed to correct that mistake. She decided to accept her parents' advice and get help.

Lee spent the next year using *methadone* under medical supervision before she finally got well. She spent a lot of time studying and improved her grades. She also joined a school-sponsored "Just Say No" club. There she made drug-free friends.

She found out the hard way that hanging out with junkies would keep her involved with drugs. She wasn't going to make that mistake again!

While Lee was recovering, Dale robbed a service station to steal money for heroin. He ended up in jail. Dale wasn't stupid enough to inject heroin into his veins. But he *was* stupid enough to continue using heroin.

Today, Lee has self-respect for breaking her connection with drugs. She learned to think about the good things in her life. She also learned to concentrate on the

Even bad choices can be turned around. Counselors can help you change your thinking and your habit.

52 | good things she can do. She feels good about helping herself.

Lee realized that she needed to become her own best friend before she could make other friends.

CHAPTER 3

Summary

*I*n Chapter 2, you read about several teen-agers and the choices they made. They didn't all make good choices all the time. There were other good choices they could have made to resist drug use.

We hope their stories give you some-thing to think about when you face peer pressure. A good example of dealing with peer pressure is "Just say No." And look-ing as if you mean it! There are other ways to avoid trouble. Leave. Ignore the person pressuring you. Joke about it. Set limits ahead of time. Make excuses.

There is no magic way to avoid peer pressure. Find a way that works for you.

The most important thing to remember about drugs is that they are not magic.

Staying away from drinking, smoking, and drugs will help you have a positive self-image.

Drugs cannot solve your problems. You must do that for yourself. And drugs won't help.

Drugs might give you a few minutes of relief. They can make you too confused or too sick to care about anything. But if you're worried, if you don't feel good about yourself, drugs won't cure that.

You need to remember that as a person you have *rights*. Protecting your mind and body is one of your rights. If you stay healthy, does it matter if you aren't "one of the group"?

Former drug users claim that they are most sorry about the damage they did to their mind and body. If you are lucky enough to be drug-free, you have made the most important good choice of your life.

But if you or your friends are involved with tobacco or drugs, it is not too late to correct that with a good choice now.

The list in the back of this book gives the phone numbers of places where you and your friends can get help if you need it.

Think about it.

Then make the choice that is best for you.

Glossary
Explaining New Words

addiction Physical or mental need for a habit-forming substance.

alcoholic Person who cannot stop drinking alcoholic beverages.

AIDS (acquired immune deficiency syndrome) A disease caused by a virus and acquired through sexual contact.

carbon monoxide A colorless, poisonous gas formed when carbon is not completely burned.

central nervous system The brain and spinal cord, which receive messages from the outside world and send messages to the muscles of the body.

crash The physical pain and mental de-
pression that follows the high of a drug.

freebase A paste of cocaine and chemicals that is smoked to give a greater
high than cocaine alone.

hooked Being addicted to alcohol or
other drugs.

joint A cigarette made of marijuana; also
called reefer.

mainline To inject a drug directly into a
vein.

methadone A man-made drug that pre-
vents the high of heroin and helps the
user stop the use of heroin.

peer pressure Urging by one's friends or
social group to undertake a particular
action.

snorting Taking a drug by inhaling it.

snuff A form of powdered tobacco that is
inhaled, chewed, or placed against the
gums.

Help List

Hot Lines

* 1-800-COCAINE
  Answers any questions about cocaine.

* 1-800-9-FRIEND
  24-Hour Prevention Crisis Hotline

Call or Write

* Al-Anon/Alateen
  Family Group Headquarters, Inc.
  P.O. Box 862, Midtown Station
  New York, NY 10018-0862
  1-800-356-9996 (United States)
  1-800-443-4525 (Canada)

- National Association for Children of   **59**
   Alcoholics
   31706 Pacific Coast Highway
   South Laguna, CA 92677
   (714) 499-3889

- Narcotics Anonymous
   World Service Office
   16155 Wyandotte Street
   Van Nuys, CA 91406

- STOPP (Students To Offset Peer
   Pressure)
   P.O. Box 103, Department S
   Hudson, NH 03051-0103

- SADD (Students Against Driving Drunk)
   Box 800
   Marlboro, MA 01750
   (508) 481-3568

Telephone Book
Yellow Pages
- Alcoholism, Drug Abuse, Counselors,
   Religious Organizations

- National Council on Alcoholism and
   Drugs (Call for free literature and
   information)
   1-800-622-2255

For Further Reading

Alexander, Clifton, MD, and Alexander, Sandy. *Kick the Drug Habit*. Tucson: Antler Publishing Corp., 1989.

Ball, Jacqueline. *Everything You Need to Know about Drug Abuse*. New York: Rosen Publishing Group, 1992.

Browne, David. *Crack and Cocaine*. New York: Gloucester Press, 1987.

Dolmetsche, Paul, and Mauricette, Gail. *Teens Talk about Drugs and Alcoholism*. Garden City, NY: Doubleday & Co., 1987.

Freeman, Jodi, MEd. *How to Drug-Proof Kids*. Albuquerque, NM: The Think Shop, 1989.

Grauer, Neil A. *Drugs and the Law*. New York: Chelsea House, 1988.

Hodgkinson, Liz. *Addictions*. New York: | **61**
    Thorsons Publishing Group, 1986.
Hyde, Margaret O. *Mind Drugs*. New
    York: Dodd, Mead & Co., 1986.
Kaplan, Leslie, *Coping with Peer Pressure*.
    New York: Rosen Publishing Group,
    1990.
Kneip, Margaret E. *Self-Control*. New
    York: Rosen Publishing Group, 1991.
Lee, Essie E. *Breaking the Connection*.
    New York: Julian Messner, 1988.
Madison, Arnold. *Drugs and You*. New
    York: Julian Messner, 1982.
Newman, Susan, *You Can Say No to a
    Drink or a Drug*. New York: The
    Putnam Group, 1986.
Ryan, Elizabeth A. *Straight Talk about
    Drugs and Alcohol*. New York: Facts on
    File, 1989.
Spence, Annette. *Substance Abuse*. New
    York: Facts on File, 1989.
Ward, Brian R. *Drugs and Drug Abuse*.
    New York: Franklin Watts, 1987.
Woods, Geraldine and Harold. *Cocaine*.
    New York: Franklin Watts, 1985.

Index

64 | *About the Authors*

Sue Hurwitz has a M.A. in education and taught every grade K–9. She is the co-author of a young adult biography, *Sally Ride: Shooting for the Stars*.

Nancy Shniderman has a B.S. in computer science and has taught computer camp for teenagers.

Photo Credits

Cover photo: Chuck Peterson
Photos on pages 2, 20, 22–23, 13, 35, 39, 42, 47, 51, 55: Michael F. O'Brien; pages 8, 26: Chris Volpe; pages 17, 19, 29, 32: Stuart Rabinowitz

Design & Production: Blackbirch Graphics, Inc.